An Animal
Easter Story

By Cassie Porter

Have you ever thought about the animals
that knew the Lord long ago?
Maybe He had some that loved Him,
it's hard for us to know.
Did He have a cat or a dog back then?
I'm sure He had some really special friends!
The ones that knew Him most of all,
I'm sure they'd come running when He'd
call!

Was Jesus' horse filled with pride?
Did he know he carried the Savior
astride?
As He got older did they see,
just how wonderful this man would be?

Have you ever thought about what
the animals saw?
When Jesus spoke were they in
awe?
So many thoughts run through my
head.
Did they listen intently to what He
said?

Do you think the lambs knew
who He was?
Did they know He came down
from above?
To save us all from our own sin.
To clean our hearts from within.

Did they stop and listed to the
stories He told?
Were they watching and waiting
for His life to unfold?

Did some find Him rather odd?
Did they know that His Father was our
God?
When He prayed for us to His Father
above,
were they filled with hope and such
great love?

What did they think when the elders
came?
Did they know that Judas was to
blame?
Were they scared for Him that day
long ago?
Or did they have peace inside,
did they know?

When they made Him carry his cross
up the hill,
did they know that this was God's
will?
Were they upset
when He stumbled and fell?
Did He know they were worried,
could He tell?

When they pushed the crown of
thorns on His head,
did they cry or get angry instead?
I think they were sad and didn't
know
why this kind man was suffering
so.

I'm sure they watched, up close
and from far.
Their heads held low, mouths
ajar.
Did they feel like this was the
end,
of this man's life, their dear
friend?

As Mary lost her Son she must have wept!
I'm sure it was difficult for her to accept.
I imagine a bunny close to Mary's side.
Would she comfort her as she cried?

Was the horse worried
as he saw the cross?
Losing this King would be such a great
loss.
And the donkey that carried Mary
before Jesus was born,
was he there too, as they started to
mourn?

Was there an elephant there that
day?
Did he look on in complete dismay?
I bet they knew that Jesus was
good.
And that taking Him away couldn't
be understood.

Was there a dog
looking on in sorrow?
As He drew his last breath, He wouldn't
be there tomorrow.
I wonder if the animals that weren't
even there
could sense the loss that seemed so
unfair.

Who stood guard that night by the tomb?
Did a mouse stand by filled with gloom?
Maybe he was worried that they killed the King.
The One who would Salvation bring.

I bet the Lion stood guard that night.
His mighty roar ready for a fight.
No one would disturb the King's
sleep.
I bet he made sure all was quiet,
not a peep.

Were the stars bright that night in the sky?
As God looked down, His Son to die.
Did the camel that was gazing at the sky above,
know that this was a display of love?

Did the bear want to sleep those next few
days?
Was it like they were waiting, in a haze?
They didn't know what to expect,
those days in between, some wept!

Who was the first to see the empty
tomb?
Was it the lion, or maybe a racoon.
Did he happen upon the cloths that
day,
that Jesus was wrapped in,
in death He lay.

Or was it the chipmunk zooming this way and that way?
Did she catch a glimpse of the stone rolled away?
Did she know that the Son of God was alive?
Was her smile big, and her eyes wide?

I bet all of the animals that were there that day
were completely elated in their own way.
I bet they looked on, thankful,
that the King of the world had risen,
were they grateful?

When Jesus rose from the dead
the third day,
did the birds fly around Him?
What would their songs say?
Did everyone hear them
celelbrating the Son?
The One who brought forgiveness,
His job done.

And when He said, "I go to prepare a
place..."
Did they want to go too,
knowing their sins erased?
I imagine that day that He left,
the animals were happy,
no longer distressed.
I'm sure they knew they'd see Him one day.
Glad they were part
of His life in some way.

What would you have felt
if you had been there back then?
To experience God on Earth as a
man?
To watch as He grew and then gave
His life,
and see those that loved Him
filled with strife?
What would you have felt as He
rose from the grave?
Knowing He did all of that
only to save?
I imagine even the animals knew
that this great Man loved them too.

Other books in this series by Cassie Porter

Have you ever wondered what the animals thought that day? In the barn, a Savior, in a manger he lay. Have you ever wondered how they felt, the sight of a King, as Mary knelt.

A beautiful story of what the animals may have thought that blessed night. What they may have seen is amazing! I wish I had been there! To see our Savior come into the world, our King.

Other Children's books by Cassie Porter

Diversity and acceptance can be a difficult learning lesson. If You See A... teaches the lesson in a silly, goofy way.
If you come across an alligator eating a milkshake...
Sometimes it's easier to learn how to accept our differences if we think about it a different way. What if animals ate different things than what we'd expect? What if we accepted them anyway?
This book is full of beautiful images and funny rhymes. Your little ones will love looking at the pictures and hearing you read this book time and time again. Quirky yet educational.

If You Feel A...
Emotions are hard...even for adults at some times. We can go from happy to mad to excited to frustrated at the drop of a hat. And WE'VE been managing our emotions for a very long time. We expect children to manage them better than we do at times. As a child, I'm sure it's frustrating to feel these big emotions. Help your child navigate different situations by recognizing what they are, knowing it's ok, and knowing how a mindset shift or a different perspective can change a lot of these "feelings".
Ultimately, having our children recognizing these feelings in others and helping others with their own feelings would make us parents proud!
Kindness is always the bar!

We've all heard the poem! What are girls made of? Sugar and Spice and everything nice. That's what girls are made of. But that's not all girls are made of. This book is a celebration of our girls. Each one unique, full of character, grit, fight and grace. It's hard being a girl! But it's also such an amazing thing! Celebrate her! In all her unique qualities!

This book is full of beautiful pictures of girls, both girly girls and tomboys. It's ok to be one, or the other, or both! Show your daughter that you appreciate who she is, and that she's special!

Have you ever fallen asleep and dreamed of the silliest, wackiest, craziest superheroes you've ever seen? Charlie does! Every night Charlie goes to sleep excited to meet a new superhero.

Join Charlie as he laughs and giggles his way through each superhero and their unique powers. You'll love these heroes as much as Charlie does!

Growing up is hard! All the emotions, feelings, girl drama and hormones are difficult to navigate. For most, we feel uncomfortable with our changing bodies and like others look at us like we look at ourselves. Then there are the girls that exude confidence. How do they get that way? How do they feel confident when I feel so uncomfortable? For some it comes naturally. For others they need help with support from those around them to know how to accept themselves and build the confidence they want to have. I wrote this book for my daughters. To help remind them that they are beautiful! They are perfect just the way they were created. They are intelligent, strong, talented and driven. They are perfect!

In this book you'll find...
- Reminders of a girls beauty and attributes that make her unique. Things they can refer back to when they need encouragement in different areas.
- Pages for coloring
- Word searches, Crosswords, Word Scrambles and Missing Vowels.
- A letter to your girl, telling her just how special she is.
- 120 pages with key/answers to puzzles
I hope this book can help encourage your special girl on her journey to becoming the strong, self confident young lady that she is meant to be.

Made in the USA
Coppell, TX
24 March 2025

47521195R00033